33 Days …
with St. Joseph

To ask the Holy Spirit to help us have the
father's heart of Joseph!

Based on the Apostolic Letter *Patris Corde*
of Pope Francis (Dec 8, 2020).

Prepared by Fr. Nicholas Cachia

En Route Books and Media, LLC
St. Louis, MO

✹ENROUTE
Make the time

En Route Books and Media, LLC

5705 Rhodes Avenue

St. Louis, MO 63109

ISBN 13: 978-1-952464-59-1

and 978-1-952464-61-4

LCCN: 2021932432

Table of Contents

Introduction

These past few years I have grown in my devotion to St. Joseph, primarily because the Lord called me to become a member of the IPF Priests of St. Joseph, a group of diocesan priests dedicated to the spiritual formation of diocesan seminarians and priests. What really strikes me in this silent but most eloquent saint is his total and serene surrender to the will of God in his life.

When on December 8, 2020, Pope Francis published his Apostolic Letter *Patris Corde*, I was immediately struck by its depth. The different elements of fatherhood which the Holy Father highlights have truly spoken to my heart and I found myself desiring all the more to have that same heart of a father as St. Joseph.

In 2020, I did the consecration to St. Joseph following the book *Consecration to St. Joseph: The Wonders of Our Spiritual Father* by Fr. Donald H. Calloway, MIC (Marian Press, Stockbridge, OH, 2020). Once I prayed with the Apostolic Letter of Pope Francis, I found myself drawn to propose a simple prayerful resource for a deeper intimate relationship with St. Joseph. Thus, this small book was born.

The aim of the book is very simple! It is a resource for meditative prayer. For each day, a grace is proposed inspired by a section of *Patris Corde*. A biblical reading is suggested for each day, helping the person to appropriate the message on a deeper level after having listened to and prayed with God's Word. Some days, the section chosen from *Patris Corde* is complemented by quotes from saints or from the teachings of recent Popes.

Why 33 days? The inspiration comes from the *True Devotion to Mary of St. Louis*

Marie de Montfort, who proposes a journey of 33 days for one's total consecration to the Divine Wisdom through Mary.

While there are two excellent starts dates for this consecration, namely February 15, culminating in the Solemnity of St. Joseph on March 19, and March 30, culminating in the Feast of St. Joseph the Worker on May 1, one should feel free to start on any day of the year with the intention of completing the consecration 33 days later.

I pray that the Holy Spirit form in the heart of the reader the same attitudes and sentiments that were in the heart of St. Joseph, whose life centered on the lives of the precious gifts that the Father entrusted into his hands: the Blessed Virgin Mary and Jesus, the Incarnate Son of God.

Day 1

Grace for the day: *That I may discover and come to love God's calling to me more, while acknowledging my smallness and hidden-ness.*

From *Patris Corde, Introduction*

"Each of us can discover in Joseph – the man who goes unnoticed, a daily, discreet and hidden presence – an intercessor, a support and a guide in times of trouble. Saint Joseph reminds us that those who appear hidden or in the shadows can play an incomparable role in the history of salvation."

SUGGESTED SCRIPTURE READING

Judges 6:11-18

YOUR PERSONAL REFLECTION

Day 2

Grace for the day: *That my "yes" to the Lord may become more total, encompassing all of myself without reservation or compromise.*

From *Patris Corde, A beloved Father*

Saint Paul VI pointed out that Joseph concretely expressed his fatherhood "by making his life a sacrificial service to the mystery of the incarnation and its redemptive purpose. He employed his legal authority over the Holy Family to devote himself completely to them in his life and work. He turned his human vocation to domestic love into a superhuman oblation of himself, his heart and all his abilities, a love placed at the service of the Messiah who was growing to maturity in his home" (Homily, 19 March 1966).

SUGGESTED SCRIPTURE READING

Matthew 1:1-16

YOUR PERSONAL REFLECTION

Day 3

Grace for the day: *That I may grow in my devotion to St. Joseph, having the same attitudes that Jesus had toward him.*

From *Patris Corde*, A beloved father

Thanks to his role in salvation history, Saint Joseph has always been venerated as a father by the Christian people… Innumerable holy men and women were passionately devoted to him. Among them was Teresa of Avila, who chose him as her advocate and intercessor, had frequent recourse to him and received whatever graces she asked of him. Encouraged by her own experience, Teresa persuaded others to cultivate devotion to Joseph.

COMPLEMENTARY QUOTES

"Saint Joseph's dignity springs from his privilege of being the legal father of the Incarnate Son of God. Here, then, is a man whom the Son of God calls father, one whom he [Jesus] serves and obeys and before whom he kneels for a paternal blessing" (St. Peter Julian Eymard, *Month of St. Joseph*, Cleveland, OH, Emmanuel Publications, 1948, 8).

"The reasons why St. Joseph must be considered the special patron of the Church, and the Church in turn draws exceeding hope from his care and patronage, chiefly arise from his having been the husband of Mary and the presumed father of Jesus..., Joseph was in his day the lawful and natural guardian, head and defender of the Holy Family.... It is thus fitting and most worthy of Joseph's dignity that, in the same way that he once kept unceasing holy watch over the family of Nazareth, so now does he protect and defend with his heavenly patronage the Church of Christ" (Pope Leo XIII, Encyclical Epistle *Quamquam pluries* [August 15, 1889]).

33 Days ... with St. Joseph

SUGGESTED SCRIPTURE READING

Matthew 13:53-58

YOUR PERSONAL REFLECTION

Day 4

Grace for the day: That my "yes" to the Lord may help me become less selfish and self-centered and more ready to give myself to others in service unto the end.

From *Patris Corde*, A beloved father

Popular trust in Saint Joseph is seen in the expression "Go to Joseph", which evokes the famine in Egypt, when the Egyptians begged Pharaoh for bread. He in turn replied: "Go to Joseph; what he says to you, do" (Gen 41:55). Pharaoh was referring to Joseph the son of Jacob, who was sold into slavery because of the jealousy of his brothers (cf. Gen 37:11-28) and who – according to the biblical account – subsequently became viceroy of Egypt (cf. Gen 41:41-44).

COMPLEMENTARY QUOTE

"If you want to form an idea of Saint Joseph's greatness, consider that by a divine privilege he merited to bear the title "father of Jesus". Reflect too that his own name "Joseph" means – an increase. Keeping in mind the great patriarch Joseph, sold by his brothers in Egypt, understand that our saint has inherited not only his name, but even more, his power, his innocence, and his sanctity. As the patriarch Joseph stored the wheat not for himself, but for the people in their time of need, so Joseph has received a heavenly commission to watch over the living Bread not for himself alone, but for the entire world" (St. Bernard of Clairvaux, as quoted in St. Peter Julian Eymard, *Month of St. Joseph*, Cleveland, OH, Emmanuel Publications, 1948, 7).

SUGGESTED SCRIPTURE READING

Genesis 41:53-57

YOUR PERSONAL REFLECTION

Day 5

Grace for the day: *That I may accept on the deepest level of my being how much I am loved and cared for by my heavenly Father, allowing this truth to seep into all my memories.*

From *Patris Corde,*
A tender and loving father

Joseph saw Jesus grow daily "in wisdom and in years and in divine and human favor" (Lk 2:52). As the Lord had done with Israel, so Joseph did with Jesus: he taught him to walk, taking him by the hand; he was for him like a father who raises an infant to his cheeks, bending down to him and feeding him (cf. Hos 11:3-4).

SUGGESTED SCRIPTURE READING

Hosea 11:1-9

YOUR PERSONAL REFLECTION

Day 6

Grace for the day: *That I may accept my weaknesses and limitations and open them up to the Lord's mercy, forgiveness, and power.*

From *Patris Corde*,
A tender and loving father

The history of salvation is worked out "in hope against hope" (Rom 4:18), through our weaknesses. All too often, we think that God works only through our better parts, yet most of his plans are realized in and despite our frailty. Thus Saint Paul could say: "To keep me from being too elated, a thorn was given me in the flesh, a messenger of Satan to torment me, to keep me from being too elated. Three times I appealed to the Lord about this, that it would leave me, but he said to me: 'My grace is sufficient for you, for power is made perfect in weakness'" (2 Cor 12:7-9).

> ### From *Patris Corde,*
> ### A tender and loving father

Since this is part of the entire economy of salvation, we must learn to look upon our weaknesses with tender mercy.

SUGGESTED SCRIPTURE READING

2 Cor 12:7-10

YOUR PERSONAL REFLECTION

Day 7

Grace for the day: *That I may approach God's loving mercy with confidence and that I may learn to discern well which spirit (evil or good) is behind the way I look at my sin.*

From *Patris Corde,* A tender and loving father

The evil one makes us see and condemn our frailty, whereas the Spirit brings it to light with tender love. Tenderness is the best way to touch the frailty within us. Pointing fingers and judging others are frequently signs of an inability to accept our own weaknesses, our own frailty. Only tender love will save us from the snares of the accuser (cf. Rev 12:10). That is why it is so important to encounter God's mercy, especially in the Sacrament of Reconciliation, where we experience his truth and tenderness.

From *Patris Corde,*
A tender and loving father

Paradoxically, the evil one can also speak the truth to us, yet he does so only to condemn us. We know that God's truth does not condemn, but instead welcomes, embraces, sustains and forgives us.

That truth always presents itself to us like the merciful father in Jesus' parable (cf. Lk 15:11-32). It comes out to meet us, restores our dignity, sets us back on our feet and rejoices for us, for, as the father says: "This my son was dead and is alive again; he was lost and is found" (v. 24).

SUGGESTED SCRIPTURE READING

Luke 15:11-32

YOUR PERSONAL REFLECTION

Day 8

Grace for the day: *That I may look at the different instances of my life and see God guiding me and leading me with tenderness to where I am today.*

From *Patris Corde,* A tender and loving father

Even through Joseph's fears, God's will, his history and his plan were at work. Joseph, then, teaches us that faith in God includes believing that he can work even through our fears, our frailties and our weaknesses. He also teaches us that amid the tempests of life, we must never be afraid to let the Lord steer our course. At times, we want to be in complete control, yet God always sees the bigger picture.

SUGGESTED SCRIPTURE READING

Psalm 46

YOUR PERSONAL REFLECTION

Day 9

Grace for the day: *That my obedience to God's will may be like that of St. Joseph: cheerful, prompt, simple and constant.*

From *Patris Corde,* An obedient father

As he had done with Mary, God revealed his saving plan to Joseph. He did so by using dreams, which in the Bible and among all ancient peoples, were considered a way for him to make his will known.

Joseph was deeply troubled by Mary's mysterious pregnancy. He did not want to "expose her to public disgrace", so he decided to "dismiss her quietly" (Mt 1:19).

In the first dream, an angel helps him resolve his grave dilemma: "Do not be afraid to take Mary as your wife, for the child conceived in her is from the Holy Spirit. She will bear a son, and you are to name him Jesus, for he will save his people from their sins" (Mt 1:20-21). Joseph's response was immediate:

From *Patris Corde,* An obedient father

"When Joseph awoke from sleep, he did as the angel of the Lord commanded him" (Mt 1:24). Obedience made it possible for him to surmount his difficulties and spare Mary.

In the second dream, the angel tells Joseph: "Get up, take the child and his mother, and flee to Egypt, and remain there until I tell you; for Herod is about to search for the child, to destroy him" (Mt 2:13). Joseph did not hesitate to obey, regardless of the hardship involved: "He got up, took the child and his mother by night, and went to Egypt, and remained there until the death of Herod" (Mt 2:14-15).

In Egypt, Joseph awaited with patient trust the angel's notice that he could safely return home. In a third dream, the angel told him that those who sought to kill the child were dead and ordered him to rise, take the child and his mother, and return to the land of Israel (cf. Mt 2:19-20).

From *Patris Corde,* An obedient father

Once again, Joseph promptly obeyed. "He got up, took the child and his mother, and went to the land of Israel" (Mt 2:21). During the return journey, "when Joseph heard that Archelaus was ruling over Judea in place of his father Herod, he was afraid to go there. After being warned in a dream" – now for the fourth time – "he went away to the district of Galilee. There he made his home in a town called Nazareth" (Mt 2:22-23).

The evangelist Luke, for his part, tells us that Joseph undertook the long and difficult journey from Nazareth to Bethlehem to be registered in his family's town of origin in the census of the Emperor Caesar Augustus. There Jesus was born (cf. Lk 2:7) and his birth, like that of every other child, was recorded in the registry of the Empire. Saint Luke is especially concerned to tell us that Jesus' parents observed all the prescriptions of the Law: the rites of the circumcision of Jesus, the purification of Mary after childbirth, the offering of the firstborn to God (cf. 2:21-24).

COMPLEMENTARY QUOTE

"If you want to know St. Joseph's obedience, look at how he rose at night at the angel's voice and, giving no care to hunger, hardships, or cold, went to Egypt where he led a hard life until the next command of God" (St. Joseph Sebastian Pelzcar, as quoted by Fr. Donald H. Calloway, MIC, *Consecration to St. Joseph: The Wonders of Our Spiritual Father*, Marian Press, Stockbridge, MA, 2020, 51).

SUGGESTED SCRIPTURE READINGS

Choose one of Joseph's dreams: Matthew 1:18-25; 2:13-15; 2:19-21; 2:22-23.

YOUR PERSONAL REFLECTION

Day 10

Grace for the day: *That I may always be attentive to God's will with a free and generous heart.*

From *Patris Corde,* An obedient father

In every situation, Joseph declared his own "fiat", like those of Mary at the Annunciation and Jesus in the Garden of Gethsemane.

In his role as the head of a family, Joseph taught Jesus to be obedient to his parents (cf. Lk 2:51), in accordance with God's command (cf. Ex 20:12).

COMPLEMENTARY QUOTE

"Saint Joseph was an ordinary sort of man on whom God relied on to do great things. He did exactly what the Lord wanted him to do, in each and every event that went to make up his life. That is why Scripture praises Joseph as "a just man". In Hebrew a just man means a good and faithful servant of God, someone who fulfills the divine will (Gen 7:1; 18:23-32; Ezek 18:5ff; Prov 12:10), or who is honorable and charitable toward his neighbor (cf. Tob 7:6; 9:6). So a just man is someone who loves God and proves his love by keeping God's commandments and directing his whole life towards the service of his brothers, his fellow men" (St. Josemaría Escrivá, *Christ is Passing By*, [New York, NY: Scepter, 1973, 40]).

SUGGESTED SCRIPTURE READINGS

Choose another one of the dreams of Saint Joseph: Matthew 1:18-25; 2:13-15; 2:19-21; 2:22-23.

YOUR PERSONAL REFLECTION

Day 11

Grace for the day: *That the Lord grant me the courage to live my "yes" to him to the full, even when it becomes hard and difficult.*

From *Patris Corde,* An obedient father

During the hidden years in Nazareth, Jesus learned at the school of Joseph to do the will of the Father. That will was to be his daily food (cf. Jn 4:34). Even at the most difficult moment of his life, in Gethsemane, Jesus chose to do the Father's will rather than his own, becoming "obedient unto death, even death on a cross" (Phil 2:8). The author of the Letter to the Hebrews thus concludes that Jesus "learned obedience through what he suffered" (5:8).

COMPLEMENTARY QUOTE

"The Council teaches: 'The obedience of faith' must be given to God as he reveals himself. By this obedience of faith man freely commits himself entirely to God, making 'the full submission of his intellect and will to God who reveals,' and willingly assenting to the revelation given by him" (Second Vatican II, Dogmatic Constitution *Dei Verbum*, 5). This statement, which touches the very essence of faith, is perfectly applicable to Joseph of Nazareth" (St. John Paul II, Apostolic Exhortation *Redemptoris Custos*, 4).

SUGGESTED SCRIPTURE READING

Hebrews 10:5-10

YOUR PERSONAL REFLECTION

Day 12

Grace for the day: *That I may become more aware that God wants to use my humble "yes" to bring about salvation for myself and for many others.*

From *Patris Corde,* An obedient father

All this makes it clear that "Saint Joseph was called by God to serve the person and mission of Jesus directly through the exercise of his fatherhood" and that in this way, "he co-operated in the fullness of time in the great mystery of salvation and is truly a minister of salvation." (St. John Paul II, Apostolic Exhortation *Redemptoris Custos* [15 August 1989], 8).

COMPLEMENTARY QUOTE

"Noble St. Joseph, I rejoice that God found you worthy of holding this eminent position whereby, established as the father of Jesus, you saw the one whose orders heaven and earth obey subjecting himself to your authority" (St. Alphonsus Liguori, as quoted in Andrew Doze, *Saint Joseph: Shadow of the Father*, trans. Florestine Audette, RJM, Staten Island, NY: Alba House, 1992, 19-20).

SUGGESTED SCRIPTURE READING

2 Cor 4:5-15

YOUR PERSONAL REFLECTION

Day 13

Grace for the day: *That I may learn to treat the other person with great respect, love, and sensitivity.*

From *Patris Corde,* An accepting father

Joseph accepted Mary unconditionally. He trusted in the angel's words. "The nobility of Joseph's heart is such that what he learned from the law he made dependent on charity. Today, in our world where psychological, verbal and physical violence towards women is so evident, Joseph appears as the figure of a respectful and sensitive man. Even though he does not understand the bigger picture, he makes a decision to protect Mary's good name, her dignity and her life. In his hesitation about how best to act, God helped him by enlightening his judgment" (Pope Francis, Homily at Mass and Beatifications, Villavicencio, Colombia [8 September 2017]).

COMPLEMENTARY QUOTES

"Dear brothers and sisters, I want to say to you once more from the bottom of my heart: like Joseph, do not be afraid to take Mary into your home, that is to say do not be afraid to love the Church. Mary, Mother of the Church, will teach you to follow your pastors, to love your bishops, your priests, your deacons and your catechists; to heed what they teach you and to pray for their intentions. Husbands, look upon the love of Joseph for Mary and Jesus; those preparing for marriage, treat your future spouse as Joseph did; those of you who have given yourselves to God in celibacy, reflect upon the teaching of the Church, our Mother: 'Virginity or celibacy for the sake of the Kingdom of God not only does not contradict the dignity of marriage but presupposes and confirms it. Marriage and virginity are two ways of expressing and living the one mystery of the Covenant of

God with his people'" (St. John Paul II, Apostolic Exhortation, *Redemptoris Custos*, 20).

"Once more, I wish to extend a particular word of encouragement to fathers so that they may take Saint Joseph as their model. He who kept watch over the Son of Man is able to teach them the deepest meaning of their own fatherhood. In the same way, each father receives his children from God, and they are created in God's own image and likeness. Saint Joseph was the spouse of Mary. In the same way, each father sees himself entrusted with the mystery of womanhood through his own wife. Dear fathers, like Saint Joseph, respect and love your spouse; and by your love and your wise presence, lead your children to God where they must be (cf. Lk 2:49)" (Pope Benedict XVI, Homily during the Eucharistic Celebration, Amadou Ahidjo Stadium of Yaoundé, Cameroon, 19 March 2009).

SUGGESTED SCRIPTURE READING

Ephesians 5:21-33

YOUR PERSONAL REFLECTION

Day 14

Grace for the day: *That, knowing God's infinite love for me, I may surrender myself completely into his hands at every moment of life.*

From *Patris Corde,* An accepting father

Often in life, things happen whose meaning we do not understand. Our first reaction is frequently one of disappointment and rebellion. Joseph set aside his own ideas in order to accept the course of events and, mysterious as they seemed, to embrace them, take responsibility for them and make them part of his own history. Unless we are reconciled with our own history, we will be unable to take a single step forward, for we will always remain hostage to our expectations and the disappointments that follow.

SUGGESTED SCRIPTURE READING

Jeremiah 29:10-14

YOUR PERSONAL REFLECTION

Day 15

Grace for the day: *That the Lord may grant me the gift to consider the present moment within the broader reality of his plan of salvation for me and for many others.*

From *Patris Corde,* An accepting father

The spiritual path that Joseph traces for us is not one that explains, but accepts. Only as a result of this acceptance, this reconciliation, can we begin to glimpse a broader history, a deeper meaning. We can almost hear an echo of the im-passioned reply of Job to his wife, who had urged him to rebel against the evil he endured: "Shall we receive the good at the hand of God, and not receive the bad?" (Job 2:10).

Joseph is certainly not passively resigned, but courageously and firmly proactive. In our own lives, acceptance and welcome can be an expression of the Holy Spirit's gift of fortitude.

From *Patris Corde,* An accepting father

Only the Lord can give us the strength needed to accept life as it is, with all its contradictions, frustrations and disappointments.

Jesus' appearance in our midst is a gift from the Father, which makes it possible for each of us to be reconciled to the flesh of our own history, even when we fail to understand it completely.

SUGGESTED SCRIPTURE READING

1 Kings 19:9-18

YOUR PERSONAL REFLECTION

Day 16

Grace for the day: *That the Lord may grant me the grace to believe that he is capable of ushering forth new life from death.*

From *Patris Corde,* An accepting father

Just as God told Joseph: "Son of David, do not be afraid!" (Mt 1:20), so he seems to tell us: "Do not be afraid!" We need to set aside all anger and disappointment, and to embrace the way things are, even when they do not turn out as we wish. Not with mere resignation but with hope and courage. In this way, we become open to a deeper meaning. Our lives can be miraculously reborn if we find the courage to live them in accordance with the Gospel. It does not matter if everything seems to have gone wrong or some things can no longer be fixed. God can make flowers spring up from stony ground. Even if our heart condemns us, "God is greater than our hearts, and he knows everything" (1 Jn 3:20).

33 Days ... with St. Joseph

SUGGESTED SCRIPTURE READING

Isaiah 41:8-13

YOUR PERSONAL REFLECTION

Day 17

Grace for the day: *That I may experience peace and serenity in my heart even amidst adverse and difficult circumstances.*

From *Patris Corde,* An accepting father

Reality, in its mysterious and irreducible complexity, is the bearer of existential meaning, with all its lights and shadows. Thus, the Apostle Paul can say: "We know that all things work together for good, for those who love God" (Rom 8:28). To which Saint Augustine adds, "even that which is called evil (*etiam illud quod malum dicitur*)". In this greater perspective, faith gives meaning to every event, however happy or sad.

Nor should we ever think that believing means finding facile and comforting solutions. The faith Christ taught us is what we see in Saint Joseph. He did not look for shortcuts, but confronted reality with open eyes and accepted personal responsibility for it.

Suggested Scripture Reading

Philippians 4:4-7.10-13

Your Personal Reflection

Day 18

Grace for the day: *That the Lord may touch my heart as to be sensitive to the needs of others, even before I am told anything.*

From *Patris Corde*, An accepting father

Joseph's attitude encourages us to accept and welcome others as they are, without exception, and to show special concern for the weak, for God chooses what is weak (cf. 1 Cor 1:27). He is the "Father of orphans and protector of widows" (Ps 68:6), who commands us to love the stranger in our midst. I like to think that it was from Saint Joseph that Jesus drew inspiration for the parable of the prodigal son and the merciful father (cf. Lk 15:11-32).

SUGGESTED SCRIPTURE READING

1 Corinthians 9:19-23

Y*OUR* P*ERSONAL* R*EFLECTION*

Day 19

Grace for the day: *That, whatever the circumstance, I may always rely on God's constant loving presence and guidance with creative courage.*

> From *Patris Corde,*
> A creatively courageous father

If the first stage of all true interior healing is to accept our personal history and embrace even the things in life that we did not choose, we must now add another important element: creative courage. This emerges especially in the way we deal with difficulties. In the face of difficulty, we can either give up and walk away, or somehow engage with it. At times, difficulties bring out resources we did not think we had.

SUGGESTED SCRIPTURE READING

Luke 21:10-19

Your Personal Reflection

Day 20

Grace for the day: *That I may learn to put my gifts and natural faculties at God's disposal.*

> From *Patris Corde,*
> A creatively courageous father

God acts through events and people. Joseph was the man chosen by God to guide the beginnings of the history of redemption. He was the true "miracle" by which God saves the child and his mother. God acted by trusting in Joseph's creative courage. Arriving in Bethlehem and finding no lodging where Mary could give birth, Joseph took a stable and, as best he could, turned it into a welcoming home for the Son of God come into the world (cf. Lk 2:6-7). Faced with imminent danger from Herod, who wanted to kill the child, Joseph was warned once again in a dream to protect the child, and rose in the middle of the night to prepare the flight into Egypt (cf. Mt 2:13-14).

COMPLEMENTARY QUOTE

"I live much *more* in God's will when I do the little, ordinary work he gives me to do right now. Yes, the more consciously I live and the more concentrated I am in the moment, the more I am one with God's will. It is in the very smallest things that I meet the very greatest… If only we could understand that we can only realize our dream by being totally present to the little and insignificant things we have to do at each moment. We encounter the infinity of God only in the present moment. The more we are recollected in the moment, the more clearly does the eternal now of God reveal itself… The present moment is the incarnation of God's eternity" (Wilfrid Stinissen, *Into Your Hands, Father. Abandoning Ourselves to the God who Loves Us*, Ignatius, San Francisco, 2011, 61).

SUGGESTED SCRIPTURE READING

Luke 2:1-7

YOUR PERSONAL REFLECTION

Day 21

Grace for the day: *That I may use my intelligence and creativity, open to the guidance of the Holy Spirit, to serve God's saving plan.*

> ### From *Patris Corde,*
> ### A creatively courageous father

God always finds a way to carry out his saving plan … God always finds a way to save us, provided we show the same creative courage as the carpenter of Nazareth, who was able to turn a problem into a possibility by trusting always in divine providence.

If at times God seems not to help us, surely this does not mean that we have been abandoned, but instead are being trusted to plan, to be creative, and to find solutions ourselves.

> ### From *Patris Corde,*
> ### A creatively courageous father

That kind of creative courage was shown by the friends of the paralytic, who lowered him from the roof in order to bring him to Jesus (cf. Lk 5:17-26). Difficulties did not stand in the way of those friends' boldness and persistence.

They were convinced that Jesus could heal the man, and "finding no way to bring him in because of the crowd, they went up on the roof and let him down with his bed through the tiles into the middle of the crowd in front of Jesus. When he saw their faith, he said, 'Friend, your sins are forgiven you'" (vv. 19-20). Jesus recognized the creative faith with which they sought to bring their sick friend to him.

SUGGESTED SCRIPTURE READING

Luke 5:17-26

Your Personal Reflection

Day 22

Grace for the day: *That I may promptly do whatever I understand the Lord is asking of me with simplicity and alacrity.*

> From *Patris Corde,*
> A creatively courageous father

At the end of every account in which Joseph plays a role, the Gospel tells us that he gets up, takes the child and his mother, and does what God commanded him (cf. Mt 1:24; 2:14.21). Indeed, Jesus and Mary his Mother are the most precious treasure of our faith.

COMPLEMENTARY QUOTE

"For a Christian who wishes to distinguish himself before God, there is always the possibility of trying to do great things on one's own, but that does not go very far. True growth consists in placing oneself, without reserve, at the disposal of the Lord's will, which is still unknown. This form of readiness is typically Catholic. It alone brings about a complete openness... Following the Lord's example, a Catholic never chooses anything in particular. He chooses obedience and nothing more" (Adrienne von Speyr as quoted in Wilfrid Stinissen, *Into Your Hands, Father. Abandoning Ourselves to the God who Loves Us*, Ignatius, San Francisco, 2011, 56).

SUGGESTED SCRIPTURE READING

John 19:25b-27

Your Personal Reflection

Day 23

Grace for the day: *That I may grow in my love for the Church as Christ's Body and learn from St. Joseph to help her grow and to protect her from any onslaught of the evil one.*

> **From *Patris Corde*,**
> **A creatively courageous father**

We should always consider whether we ourselves are protecting Jesus and Mary, for they are also mysteriously entrusted to our own responsibility, care and safekeeping. The Son of the Almighty came into our world in a state of great vulnerability. He needed to be defended, protected, cared for and raised by Joseph. God trusted Joseph, as did Mary, who found in him someone who would not only save her life, but would always provide for her and her child.

From *Patris Corde,*
A creatively courageous father

In this sense, Saint Joseph could not be other than the Guardian of the Church, for the Church is the continuation of the Body of Christ in history, even as Mary's motherhood is reflected in the motherhood of the Church. In his continued protection of the Church, Joseph continues to protect *the child and his mother*, and we too, by our love for the Church, continue to love *the child and his mother.*

SUGGESTED SCRIPTURE READING

Deuteronomy 32:9-14

YOUR PERSONAL REFLECTION

Day 24

Grace for the day: *That my eyes may be more open to see and serve Christ in those who are most in need.*

> From *Patris Corde,*
> A creatively courageous father

That child would go on to say: "As you did it to one of the least of these who are members of my family, you did it to me" (Mt 25:40). Consequently, every poor, needy, suffering or dying person, every stranger, every prisoner, every infirm person is "the child" whom Joseph continues to protect. For this reason, Saint Joseph is invoked as protector of the unfortunate, the needy, exiles, the afflicted, the poor and the dying. Consequently, the Church cannot fail to show a special love for the least of our brothers and sisters, for Jesus showed a particular concern for them and personally identified with them. From Saint Joseph, we must learn that same care and responsibility.

From *Patris Corde,*
A creatively courageous father

We must learn to love the child and his mother, to love the sacraments and charity, to love the Church and the poor. Each of these realities is always the child and his mother.

SUGGESTED SCRIPTURE READING

Matthew 25:31-46

YOUR PERSONAL REFLECTION

Day 25

Grace for the day: *That I learn to appreciate and savor more how work helps the human person bring forth his beautiful potential for the glory of God and the service of others.*

From *Patris Corde*, A working father

There is a renewed need to appreciate the importance of dignified work, of which Saint Joseph is an exemplary patron.

Work is a means of participating in the work of salvation, an opportunity to hasten the coming of the Kingdom, to develop our talents and abilities, and to put them at the service of society and fraternal communion. It becomes an opportunity for the fulfilment not only of oneself, but also of that primary cell of society which is the family. A family without work is particularly vulnerable to difficulties, tensions, estrangement and even break-up. How can we speak of human dignity without working to ensure that everyone is able to earn a decent living?

COMPLEMENTARY QUOTE

"Work was the daily expression of love in the life of the Family of Nazareth. The Gospel specifies the kind of work Joseph did in order to support his family: he was a carpenter. This simple word sums up Joseph's entire life. For Jesus, these were hidden years, the years to which Luke refers after recounting the episode that occurred in the Temple: 'And he went down with them and came to Nazareth, and was obedient to them' (Lk 2:51). This 'submission' or obedience of Jesus in the house of Nazareth should be understood as a sharing in the work of Joseph. Having learned the work of his presumed father, he was known as 'the carpenter's son.' If the Family of Nazareth is an example and model for human families, in the order of salvation and holiness, so too, by analogy, is Jesus' work at the side of Joseph the carpenter. In our own day, the Church has emphasized this by instituting the liturgical memorial of St.

Joseph the Worker on May 1. Human work, and especially manual labor, receive special prominence in the Gospel. Along with the humanity of the Son of God, work too has been taken up in the mystery of the Incarnation, and has also been redeemed in a special way. At the workbench where he plied his trade together with Jesus, Joseph brought human work closer to the mystery of the Redemption" (St. John Paul II, Apostolic Exhortation *Redemptoris Custos*, 22).

SUGGESTED SCRIPTURE READINGS

Deuteronomy 24:14-15; Sirach 34:22 (or 34:26-27)

YOUR PERSONAL REFLECTION

Day 26

Grace for the day: *That I do my best to see that all people have the opportunity to work and earn their living for themselves and their families.*

From *Patris Corde*, A working father

The crisis of our time, which is economic, social, cultural and spiritual, can serve as a summons for all of us to rediscover the value, the importance and necessity of work for bringing about a new "normal" from which no one is excluded. Saint Joseph's work reminds us that God himself, in becoming man, did not disdain work. The loss of employment that affects so many of our brothers and sisters, and has increased as a result of the Covid-19 pandemic, should serve as a summons to review our priorities. Let us implore Saint Joseph the Worker to help us find ways to express our firm conviction that no young person, no person at all, no family should be without work!

COMPLEMENTARY QUOTE

"Your efforts are largely concentrated on the study of new immunological and immune-chemical pathways to activate the body's own defense mechanisms or stop the proliferation of infected cells. You are also studying other specific treatments, including vaccines now being tested in clinical trials. As we know, the virus, in affecting people's health, has also affected the entire social, economic and spiritual fabric of society, paralyzing human relationships, work, manufacturing, trade and even many spiritual activities. It has an enormous impact on education. In many parts of the world, great numbers of children are unable to return to school, and this situation runs the risk of an increase in child labor, exploitation, abuse and malnutrition. In short, being unable to see a person's face and considering other people as potential carriers of the virus is a terrible metaphor of a global social crisis that must be of concern to all who have the future of humanity at heart. In this regard, none of us can fail to be concerned for the impact of the crisis on the world's poor. For many of them, the question is indeed one of survival itself" (Pope Francis, Message to the Plenary Session of the Pontifical Academy of Sciences, October 7, 2020).

SUGGESTED SCRIPTURE READING

Deuteronomy 14:28-29

YOUR PERSONAL REFLECTION

Day 27

Grace for the day: *That the Lord may grant me the grace to appreciate and savor more the tender love of the Heavenly Father at work in my life.*

From *Patris Corde,*
A father in the shadows

In his relationship to Jesus, Joseph was the earthly shadow of the heavenly Father: he watched over him and protected him, never leaving him to go on his own way. We can think of Moses' words to Israel: "In the wilderness… you saw how the Lord your God carried you, just as one carries a child, all the way that you travelled" (Deut 1:31). In a similar way, Joseph acted as a father for his whole life.

Fathers are not born, but made. A man does not become a father simply by bringing a child into the world, but by taking up the responsibility to care for that child.

From *Patris Corde,*
A father in the shadows

Whenever a man accepts responsibility for the life of another, in some way he becomes a father to that person.

SUGGESTED SCRIPTURE READING

Isaiah 43:1-7

YOUR PERSONAL REFLECTION

Day 28

Grace for the day: *That I may learn from St. Joseph how to help others grow and find their place in life.*

From *Patris Corde,*
A father in the shadows

Children today often seem orphans, lacking fathers. The Church too needs fathers. Saint Paul's words to the Corinthians remain timely: "Though you have countless guides in Christ, you do not have many fathers" (1 Cor 4:15). Every priest or bishop should be able to add, with the Apostle: "I became your father in Christ Jesus through the Gospel" (ibid.). Paul likewise calls the Galatians: "My little children, with whom I am again in travail until Christ be formed in you!" (4:19).

Being a father entails introducing children to life and reality. Not holding them back, being overprotective or possessive, but rather making them capable of deciding for themselves, enjoying freedom and exploring new possibilities.

From *Patris Corde,*
A father in the shadows

Perhaps for this reason, Joseph is traditionally called a "most chaste" father. That title is not simply a sign of affection, but the summation of an attitude that is the opposite of possessiveness. Chastity is freedom from possessiveness in every sphere of one's life. Only when love is chaste, is it truly love. A possessive love ultimately becomes dangerous: it imprisons, constricts and makes for misery. God himself loved humanity with a chaste love; he left us free even to go astray and set ourselves against him. The logic of love is always the logic of freedom, and Joseph knew how to love with extraordinary freedom. He never made himself the center of things. He did not think of himself, but focused instead on the lives of Mary and Jesus.

Suggested Scripture Reading

Galatians 4:12-20

YOUR PERSONAL REFLECTION

Day 29

Grace for the day: *That, like St. Joseph, I may grow in my self-gift with great generosity of heart.*

> ### From *Patris Corde,*
> ### A father in the shadows

Joseph found happiness not in mere self-sacrifice but in self-gift. In him, we never see frustration but only trust. His patient silence was the prelude to concrete expressions of trust. Our world today needs fathers. It has no use for tyrants who would domineer others as a means of compensating for their own needs. It rejects those who confuse authority with authoritarianism, service with servility, discussion with oppression, charity with a welfare mentality, power with destruction. Every true vocation is born of the gift of oneself, which is the fruit of mature sacrifice. The priesthood and consecrated life likewise require this kind of maturity.

From *Patris Corde,*
A father in the shadows

Whatever our vocation, whether to marriage, celibacy or virginity, our gift of self will not come to fulfilment if it stops at sacrifice; were that the case, instead of becoming a sign of the beauty and joy of love, the gift of self would risk being an expression of unhappiness, sadness and frustration.

SUGGESTED SCRIPTURE READING

Acts 20:17-35

YOUR PERSONAL REFLECTION

Day 30

Grace for the day: *That I may know when I am needed and when it's time for me to move out of the way for others to blossom.*

From *Patris Corde,*
A father in the shadows

When fathers refuse to live the lives of their children for them, new and unexpected vistas open up. Every child is the bearer of a unique mystery that can only be brought to light with the help of a father who respects that child's freedom. A father who realizes that he is most a father and educator at the point when he becomes "useless", when he sees that his child has become independent and can walk the paths of life unaccompanied. When he becomes like Joseph, who always knew that his child was not his own but had merely been entrusted to his care. In the end, this is what Jesus would have us understand when he says: "Call no man your father on earth, for you have one Father, who is in heaven" (Mt 23:9).

33 Days … with St. Joseph

SUGGESTED SCRIPTURE READING

Colossians 3:20-21

YOUR PERSONAL REFLECTION

Day 31

Grace for the day: *That, like St. Joseph, I may always keep in mind that, in my relations with others, I am always called to be a "sign" pointing to the greater fatherhood of God.*

In every exercise of our fatherhood, we should always keep in mind that it has nothing to do with possession, but is rather a "sign" pointing to a greater fatherhood. In a way, we are all like Joseph: a shadow of the heavenly Father, who "makes his sun rise on the evil and on the good, and sends rain on the just and on the unjust" (Mt 5:45). And a shadow that follows his Son.

Suggested Scripture Reading

Matthew 23:1-12

YOUR PERSONAL REFLECTION

Day 32

Grace for the day: *That, like St. Joseph, I may seek to grow in holiness by placing my life entirely in the hands of the Father's providence.*

From *Patris Corde*, Conclusion

The aim of this Apostolic Letter is to increase our love for this great saint, to encourage us to implore his intercession and to imitate his virtues and his zeal. ...

The saints help all the faithful "to strive for the holiness and the perfection of their particular state of life" (Second Vatican Council, Dogmatic Constitution *Lumen Gentium*, 42). Their lives are concrete proof that it is possible to put the Gospel into practice.

COMPLEMENTARY QUOTE

"Do not be afraid to set your sights higher, to allow yourself to be loved and liberated by

God. Do not be afraid to let yourself be guided by the Holy Spirit. Holiness does not make you less human, since it is an encounter between your weakness and the power of God's grace. For in the words of León Bloy, when all is said and done, 'the only great tragedy in life, is not to become a saint'" (Pope Francis, Apostolic Exhortation *Gaudete et Exsultate*, 2018, 34).

SUGGESTED SCRIPTURE READING

Philippians 4:8-9

Your Personal Reflection

Day 33

Grace for the day: *That I may always put myself under the protection of St. Joseph and share in his creative faithfulness as I move forward in life with great faith.*

From *Patris Corde*, Final Prayer

Hail, Guardian of the Redeemer,
Spouse of the Blessed Virgin Mary.
To you God entrusted his only Son;
in you Mary placed her trust;
with you Christ became man.

Blessed Joseph, to us too,
show yourself a father
and guide us in the path of life.
Obtain for us grace, mercy and courage,
and defend us from every evil. Amen.

St. Joseph, Father of the Interior Life, obtain for us the virtues of your heart, simplicity, detachment and love of the hidden life. (Said daily by the IPF Priests of St. Joseph.)

SUGGESTED SCRIPTURE READING

Psalm 111

YOUR PERSONAL REFLECTION

ABOUT THE AUTHOR

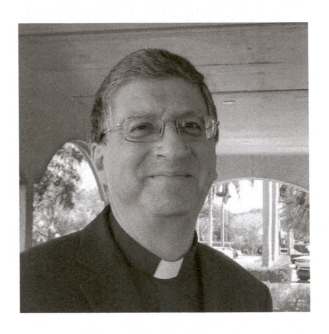

Fr. Nicholas Cachia is a priest of the Arch-diocese of Malta, now serving at St. Vincent de Paul Regional Seminary in Florida. Fr. Cachia has long been associated with the Institute for Priestly Formation and since 2018, he has been an external member of the IPF Priests of St. Joseph.

ABOUT THE COVER
ILLUSTRATION

Nathanael Theuma, 2018, Private Collection (with the author's permission)

Author's description of painting: I love presenting Joseph with the Torah in his hands. Like any father in Israel, he had the mission to give his son not only stability of house and generation (from the house of David), but also to give him identity and personality. Inspired by the faith of the fathers, he formed in Jesus a character of great humanity and phenomenal sensitivity. I believe that the way that the adult Jesus looked upon others, upon their needs, how he treated women, religion, faith, the values of obedience, of listening, of faith ... all this he received from his father. Thus, within the written word, which Joseph is embracing, there is the Word which is the life of Jesus.

Made in USA - Kendallville, IN
1238237_9781952464614
02.23.2021 0853